KINGFISHER

Jet Airliners

Robin Kerrod

Kingfisher Books

Kingfisher Books, Grisewood & Dempsey Ltd,
Elsley House, 24–30 Great Titchfield Street,
London WIP 7AD.

First published in 1989 by Kingfisher Books
Reprinted 1990

BRITISH LIBRARY CATALOGUING IN PUBLICATION DATA
Kerrod, Robin
Jets and airliners.
1. Aeroplanes – For children
I. Title II. Series
629.133'34
ISBN 0-86272-376-0

Series editor: Jacqui Bailey
Designed by David Jefferis
Text edited by Jackie Gaff
Illustrated by Michael Roffe; Peter Bull;
Peter Chesterton; Drawing Attention;
Peter Stephenson/*Jillian Burgess*

Phototypeset by Southern Positives
and Negatives (SPAN), Lingfield, Surrey
Printed in Spain

Contents

If you find an unusual or difficult word in this book, check for an explanation in the glossary on pages 30 and 31.

Cleared for Take-off

"Speedbird 610, you are cleared for take-off."
"Roger," replies the Captain of the big jet airliner waiting at the end of the runway. Keeping the brakes on, he opens the throttle. The jet engines scream as they build up power. Then the Captain releases the brakes and the airliner hurtles down the runway.

Within minutes, it is travelling fast enough to fly. The Captain gently pulls back the control column and Speedbird 610 lifts its nose and climbs high up into the sky.

Airliners are aircraft that carry passengers, and every year over 500 million people travel all over the world on them. At busy international airports, as many as 1000 airliners may take off or land every day.
Lufthansa
YT

The Jet Age

Since the first regular passenger flights began in 1914, the size of airliners has grown steadily bigger. Today, the Boeing 747 is one of the biggest airliners, carrying 394 passengers.

McDonnell Douglas DC-10 (1970) one of the first wide-bodied three-engined jets

Boeing 747 (1969) first jumbo jet

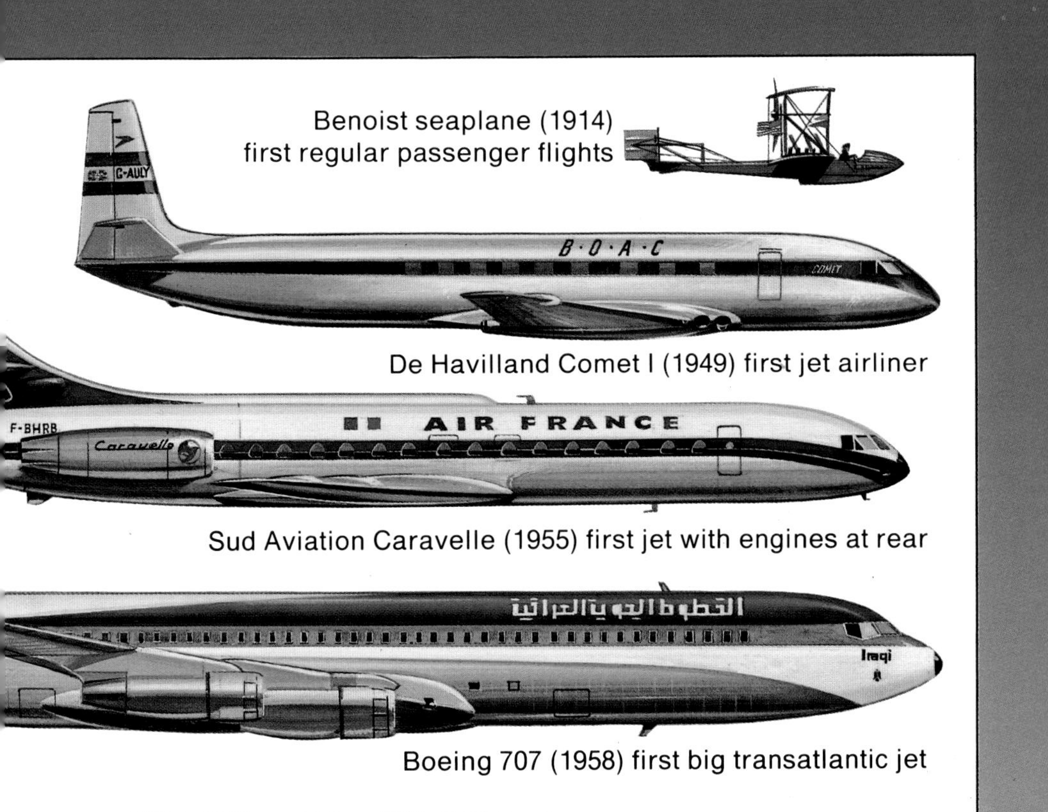

Benoist seaplane (1914) first regular passenger flights

De Havilland Comet I (1949) first jet airliner

Sud Aviation Caravelle (1955) first jet with engines at rear

Boeing 707 (1958) first big transatlantic jet

How Planes Fly

Full of passengers, a Boeing 747 jumbo jet weighs over 300 tonnes. How can anything that heavy fly? Well, it must have wings and it has to travel very fast. The shape of the wings is important. They have a special rounded shape, called an aerofoil. When wings move through the air it tries to push them upwards. This push is called lift, and the faster a plane goes, the bigger the lift becomes. When the lift is greater than its weight, the plane flies.

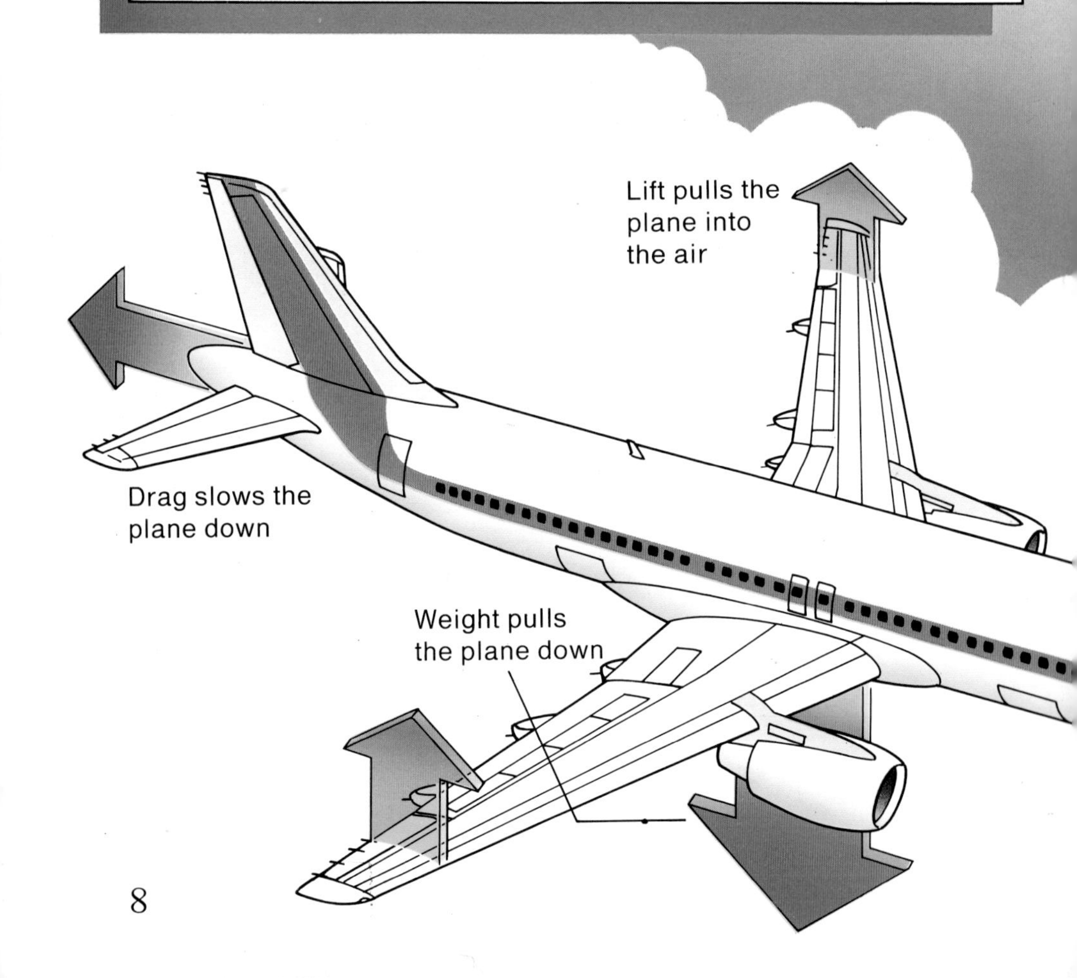

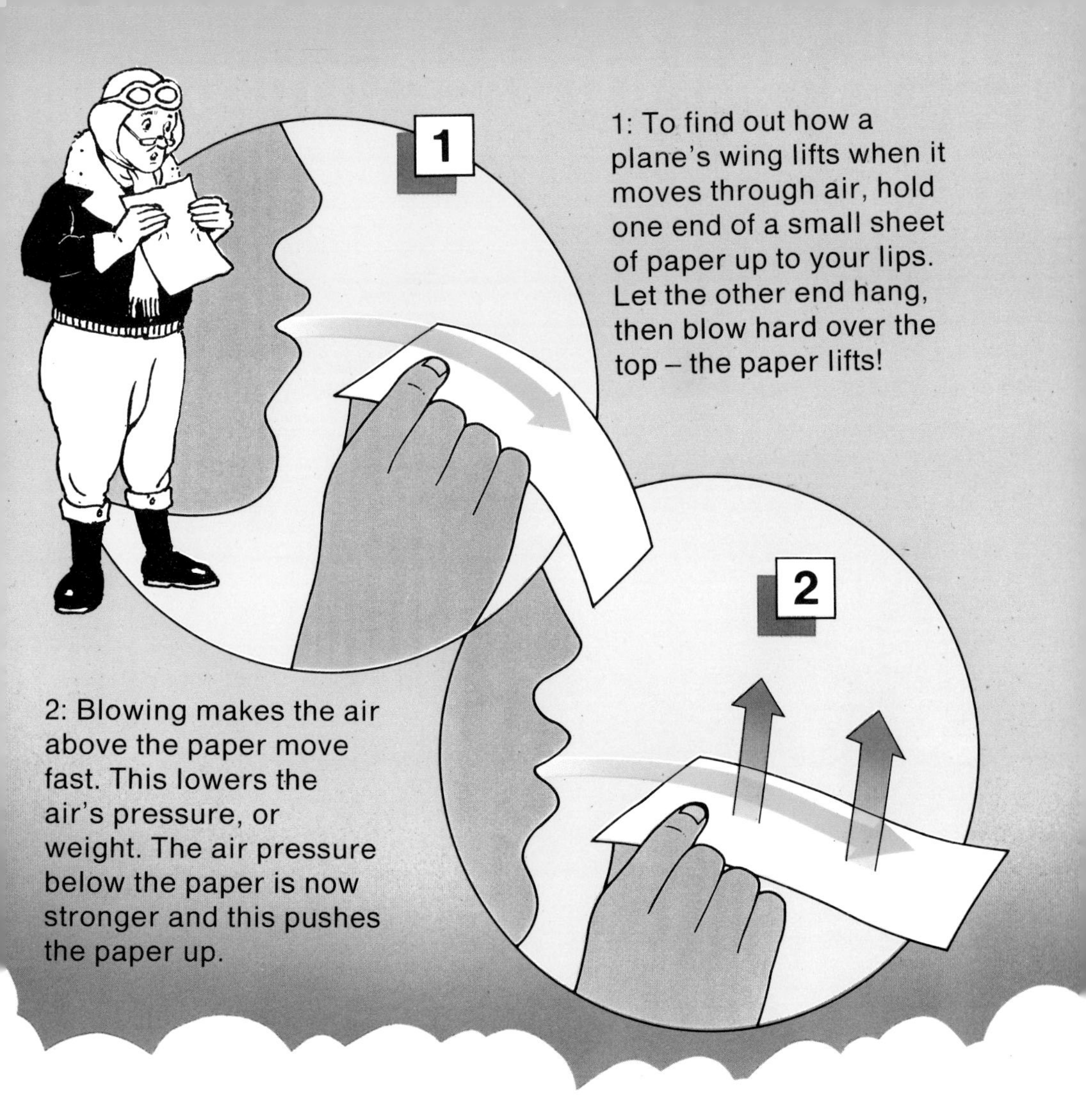

1: To find out how a plane's wing lifts when it moves through air, hold one end of a small sheet of paper up to your lips. Let the other end hang, then blow hard over the top – the paper lifts!

2: Blowing makes the air above the paper move fast. This lowers the air's pressure, or weight. The air pressure below the paper is now stronger and this pushes the paper up.

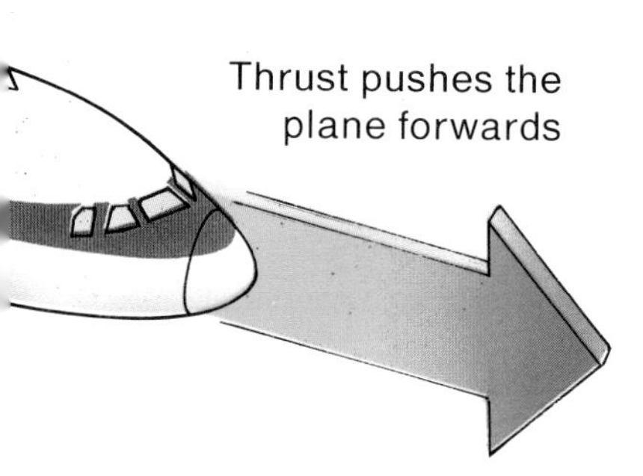

Thrust pushes the plane forwards

Four forces act on a plane when it flies. The **lift** from the air flowing past its wings balances its **weight**. **Drag** is the force of the air pushing against the plane, so the engines must produce enough **thrust** to push it forwards.

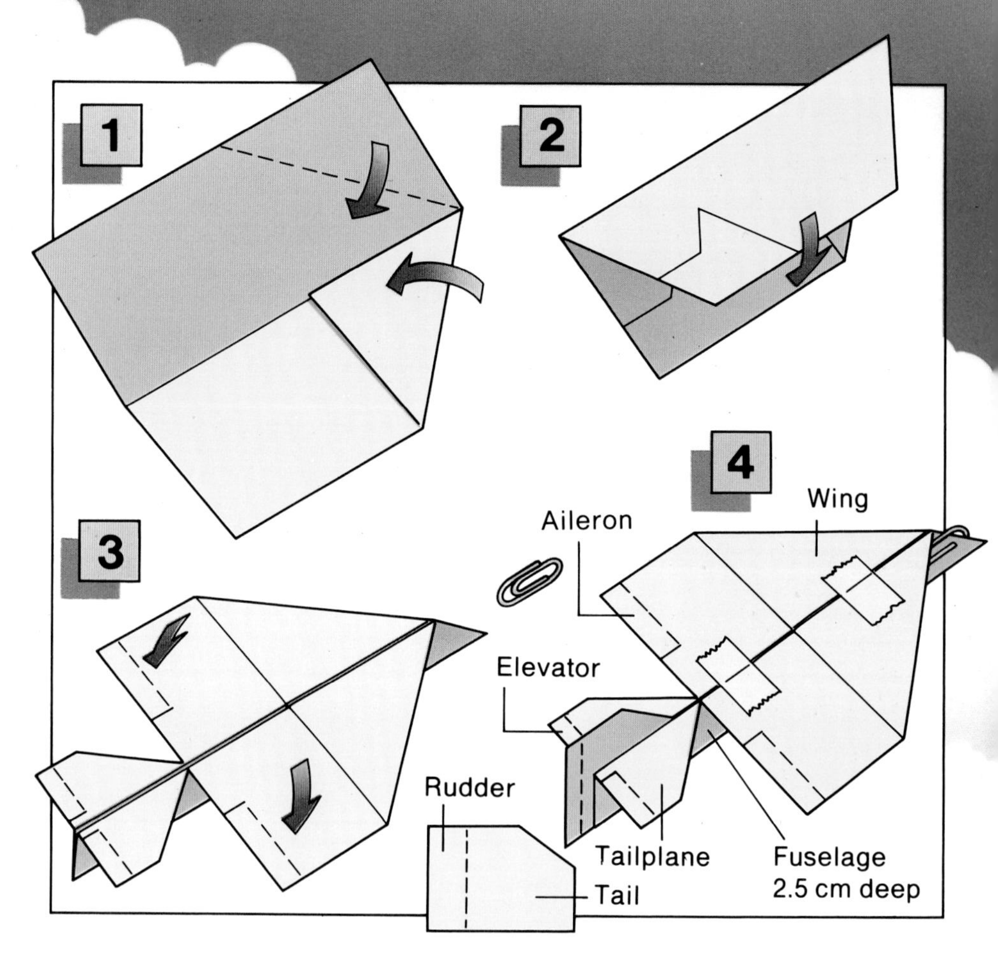

Test-fly a Glider

To make a glider, fold a square piece of stiff paper in half and turn in two corners (1). Close the paper again and fold down each side, leaving a fuselage or body about 2.5 centimetres deep (2). Cut into the paper to make wings and a tailplane, then cut and fold the elevators and ailerons (3). Weight the nose with a paperclip and use sticky tape to join the wings and tailplane. Cut a tail out of more stiff paper and make a fold for the rudder, then glue the tail into the back of your glider (4).

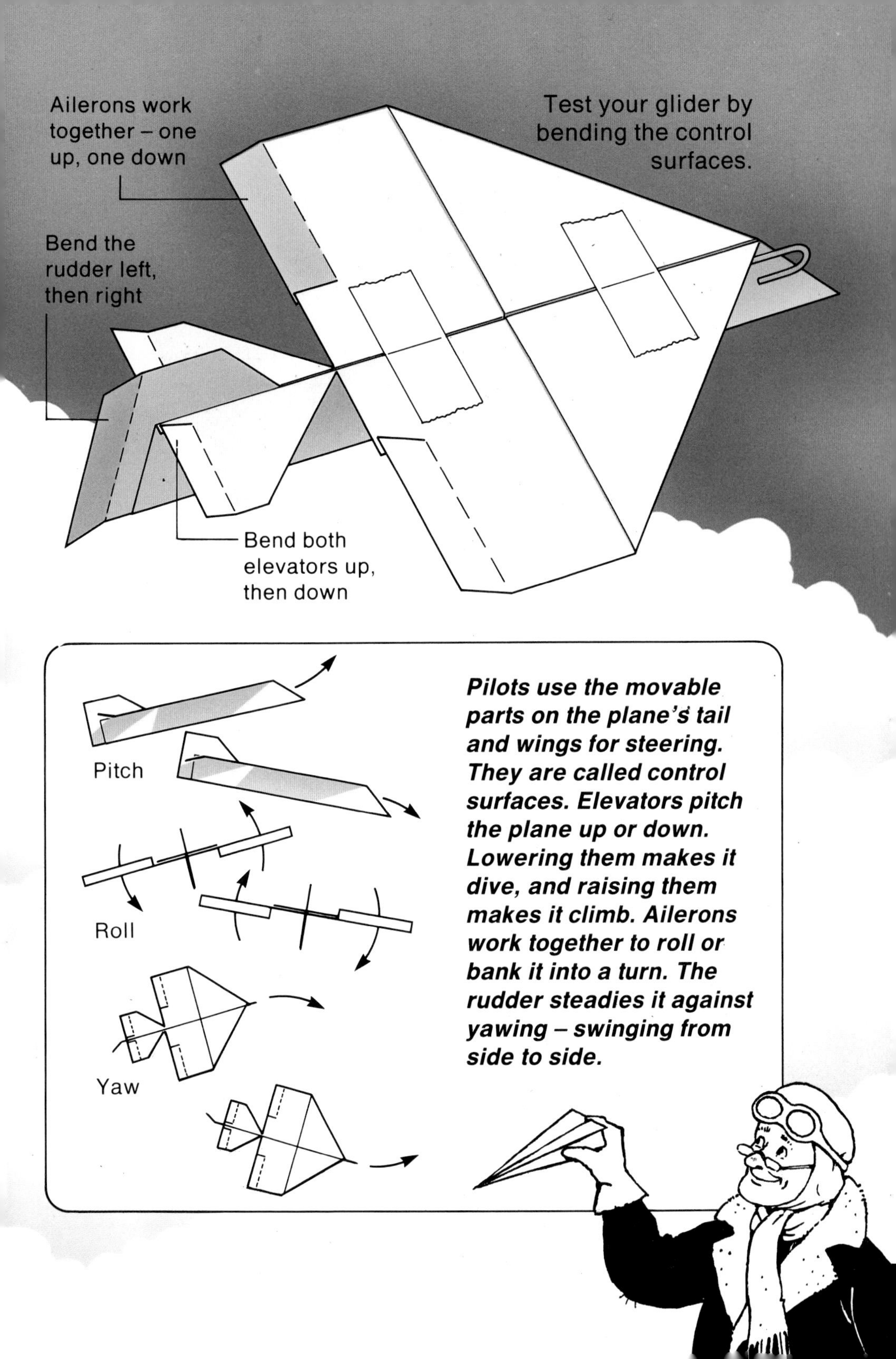

Pilots use the movable parts on the plane's tail and wings for steering. They are called control surfaces. Elevators pitch the plane up or down. Lowering them makes it dive, and raising them makes it climb. Ailerons work together to roll or bank it into a turn. The rudder steadies it against yawing – swinging from side to side.

Jet Power

The first jet plane was tested in 1939, and today most airliners have jet engines. In these engines, fuel and oxygen are burned to make a jet of hot gases. The gases shoot backwards out of the engine, producing thrust and propelling the plane forwards – rather like letting go of a blown-up balloon.

A turbofan is a very powerful type of jet engine with a huge fan in front, which sucks air into and around the engine. Turbofans can propel airliners at speeds of up to 1000 kilometres an hour.

INSIDE A TURBOFAN
In a turbofan, air (1) is sucked by the fan (2) into and around the engine. In the compressor (3), the air is packed together so that as much as possible is forced into the combustion chamber (4). Fuel is sprayed into the chamber and set alight. It burns with the oxygen in the air, producing hot gases. These roar through the turbine (5) making it spin. This drives the compressor and the fan. Thrust is produced by the escape of both the hot gases (6) and the cold air the fan sucks around the engine (7).

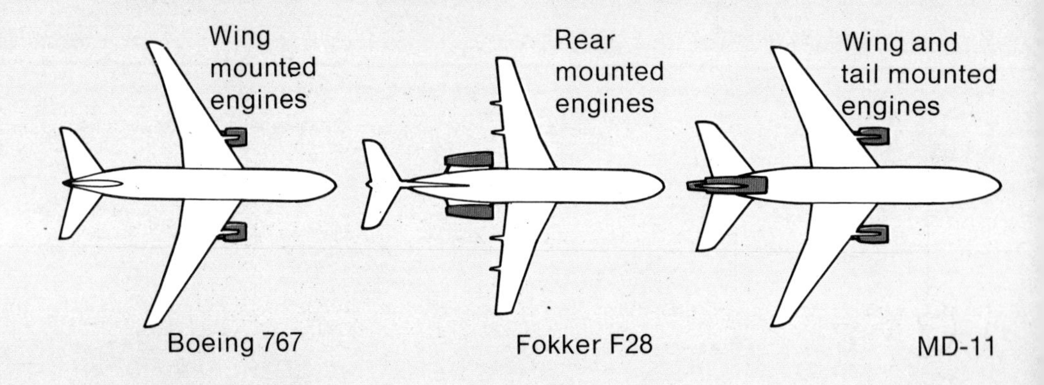

Blow up a balloon hard and pinch the neck. Then let the balloon go. With a whoosh, the air will jet backwards out of the neck. The backwards force of the escaping air sets up another force which propels the balloon forwards.

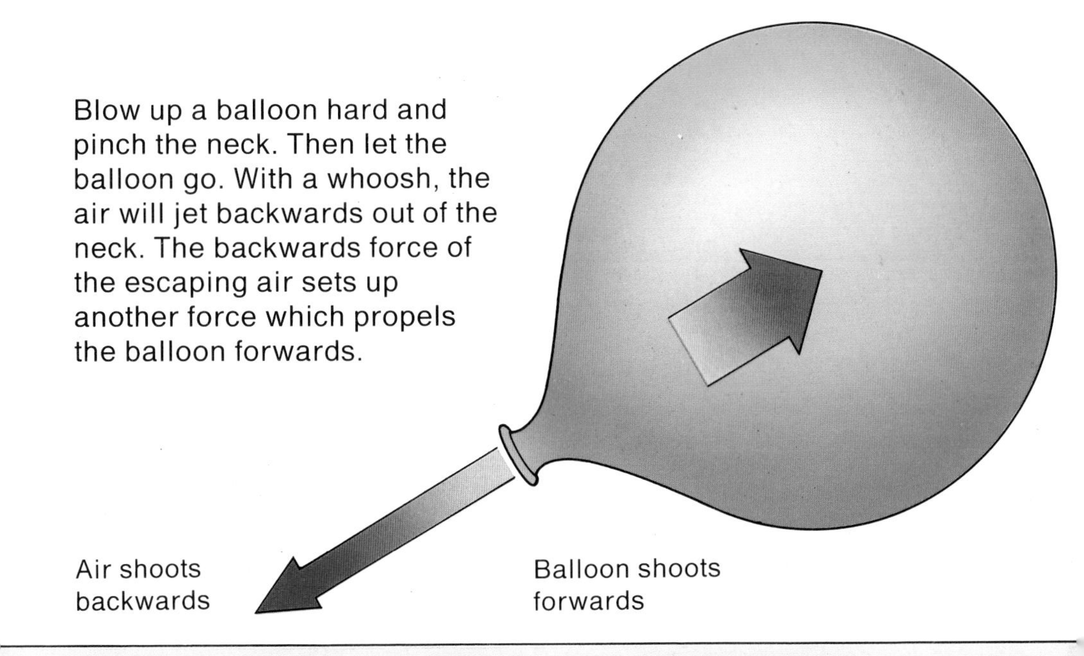

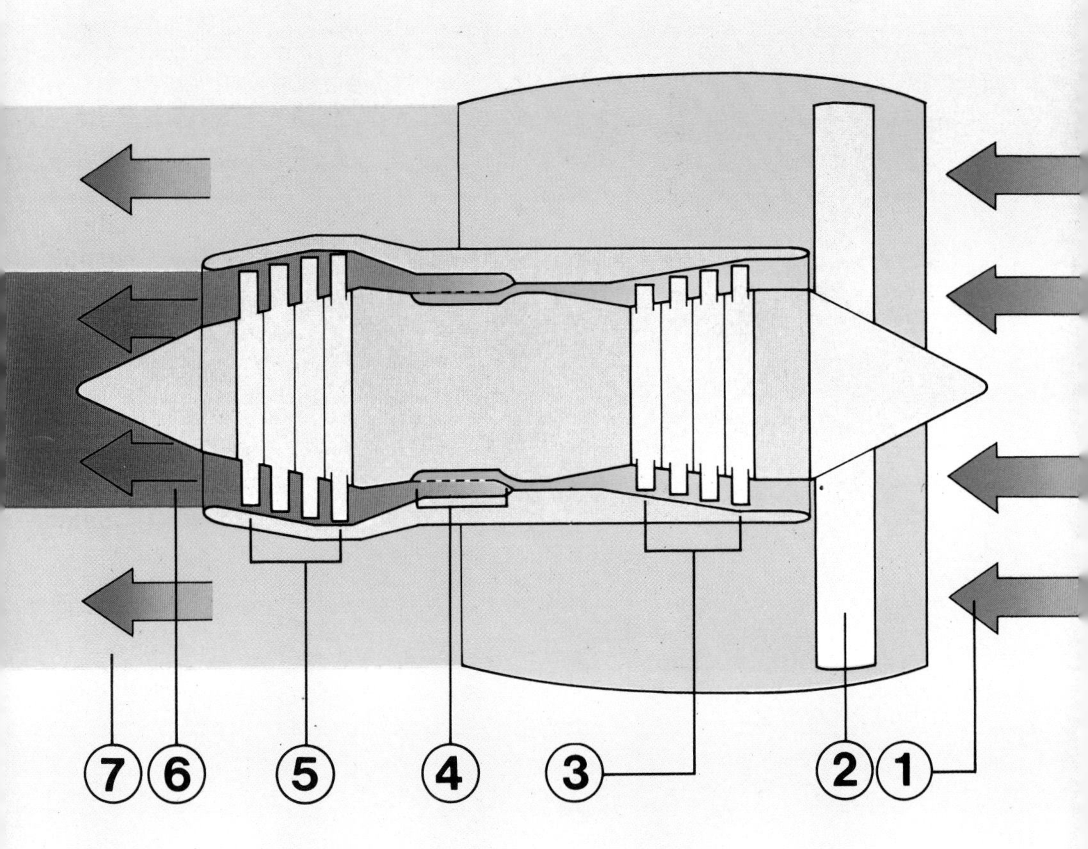

Inside an Airliner

The type of airliner used for a flight depends on how far it is travelling and how many passengers there are. Jumbo jets fly the longest distances and carry around 400 passengers. The airliner below is the Airbus A320. It flies medium-length routes and carries between 150 and 180 passengers.

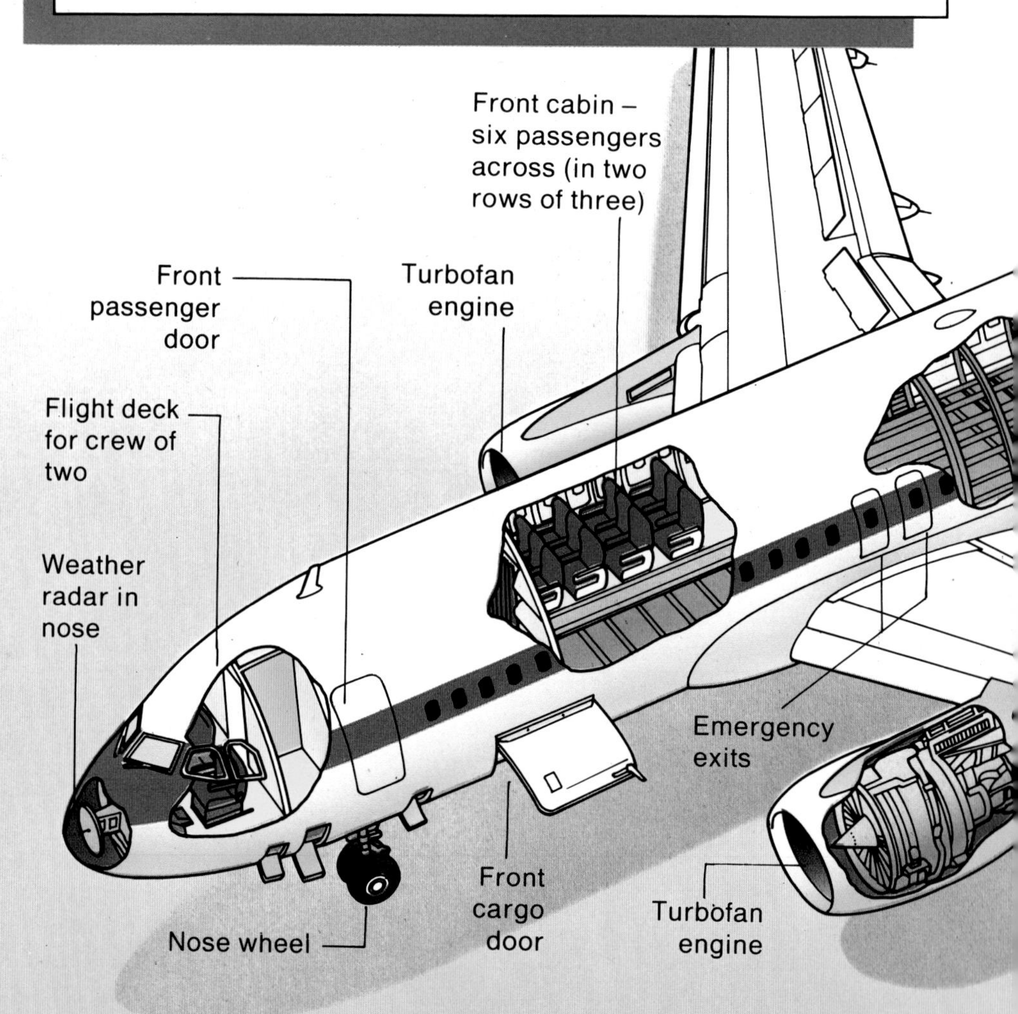

The Airbus A320 is built by a group of European companies and first flew in 1987. Its typical cruising speed is about 800 kilometres an hour.

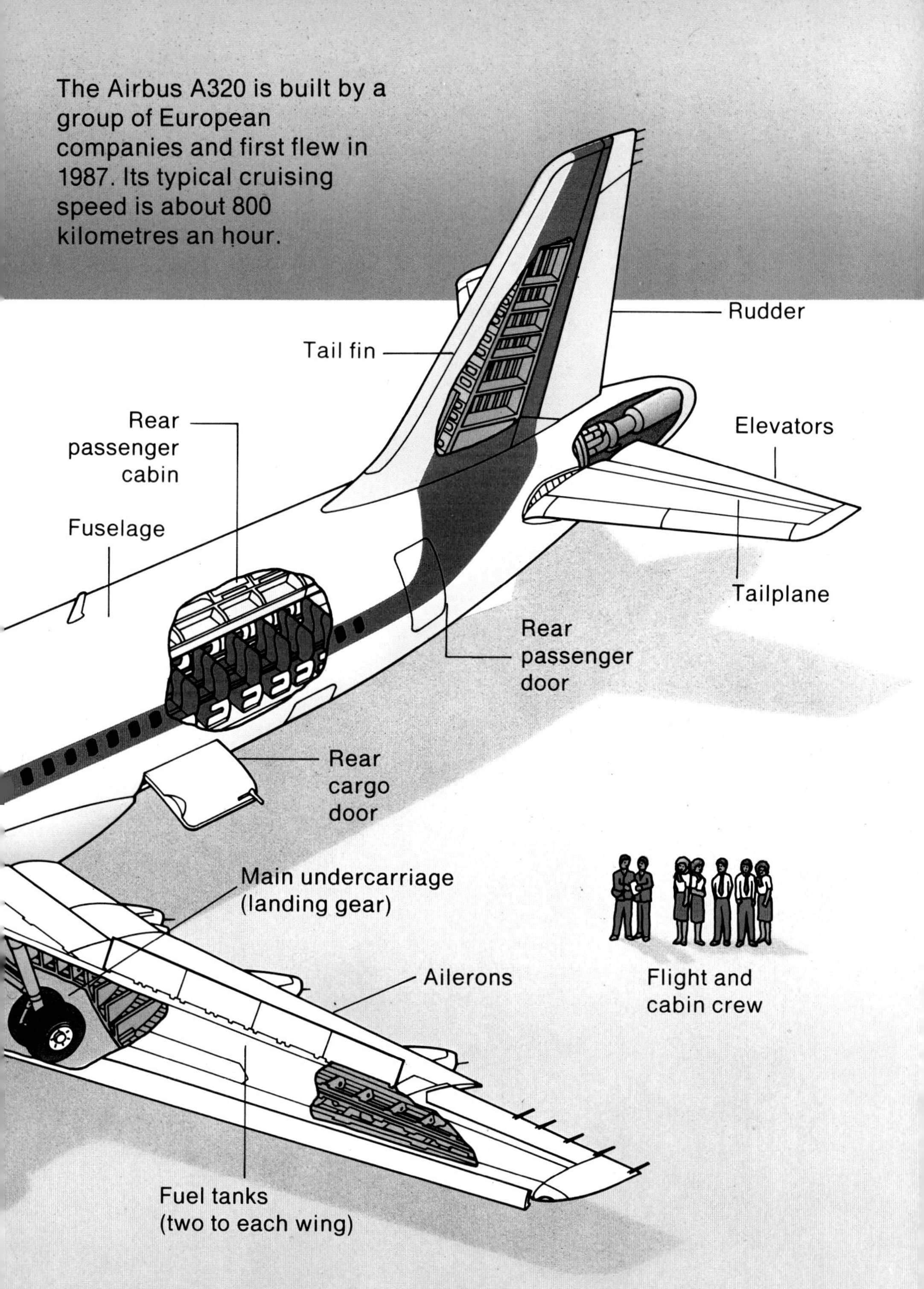

At the Controls

The flight crew of an airliner sits in the front of the plane on the flight deck. Two pilots are needed, and the Captain is the chief pilot. The pilots steer the plane with the control columns in front of them and foot pedals which move the rudder on the tail. The instruments between and in front of the Captain and co-pilot tell them what the plane is doing, so that they can fly safely and correctly.

Airspeed indicator

Altimeter

Artificial horizon

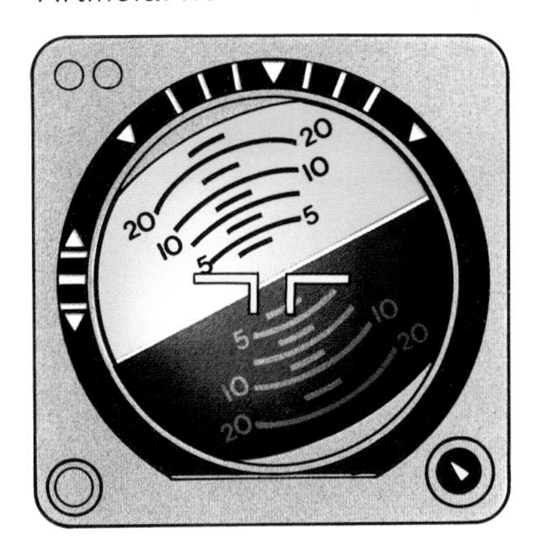

▶ These are three of the most important flight instruments. The airspeed indicator measures the plane's speed through the air in knots (1 knot equals 1.85 km/h), and the altimeter tells how high it is above sea level. The artificial horizon shows whether the plane is flying level – the yellow T-bar is the plane, and the line between blue and black marks the horizon.

At the Airport

Have you ever been abroad? Imagine you are flying to another country for a holiday. Your journey begins at the airport terminal, which is full of busy excited people. When you arrive, go first to the check-in desk for the airline company you are flying with.

Show your ticket to the person behind the check-in desk. Your name is checked against a passenger list and your suitcase is weighed. You are given a baggage tag so you can get your suitcase back when you reach your destination. The check-in person then returns your ticket and gives you a boarding card. This allows you to board, or get on, your aircraft.

READY FOR BOARDING

Your flight's departure time and the gate you will board from are shown on a screen in the terminal. Once you have your boarding card, you can go through to the departure lounge until your aircraft is ready for boarding. First, though, you have to go through passport control and security checks.

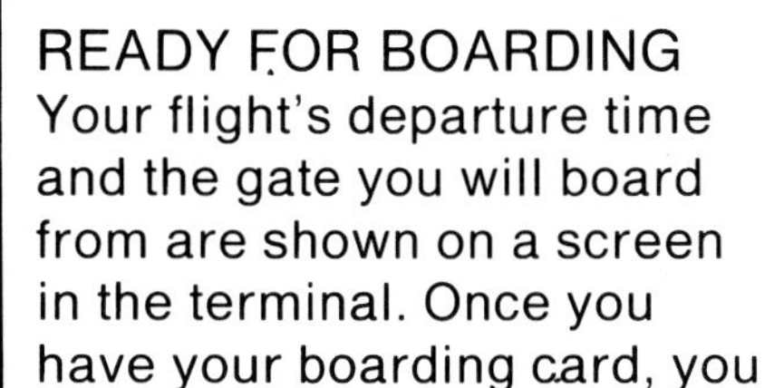

1: Check the departure time and boarding gate of your flight

2: Show your passport

3: At security, X-ray machines check you and your hand baggage for weapons and other dangerous things

4: Wait in the departure lounge until you hear your flight called

5: Show your boarding card as you get on the aircraft

A Fast Turnaround

An airport is a busy place, with planes taking off and landing all the time. An airliner must spend as little time as possible on the ground. As soon as a plane rolls to a halt outside the terminal, the ground crew gets busy. All kinds of trucks are moved in to service it, and to unload and reload it. Containers of food are brought in a catering truck, for instance. Inside the plane, workers clean the cabins and toilets and tidy up ready for the next flight to board.

Designed in the 1960s, Concorde is still the world's fastest airliner. On the ground, however, it still needs to be serviced just like any other plane.

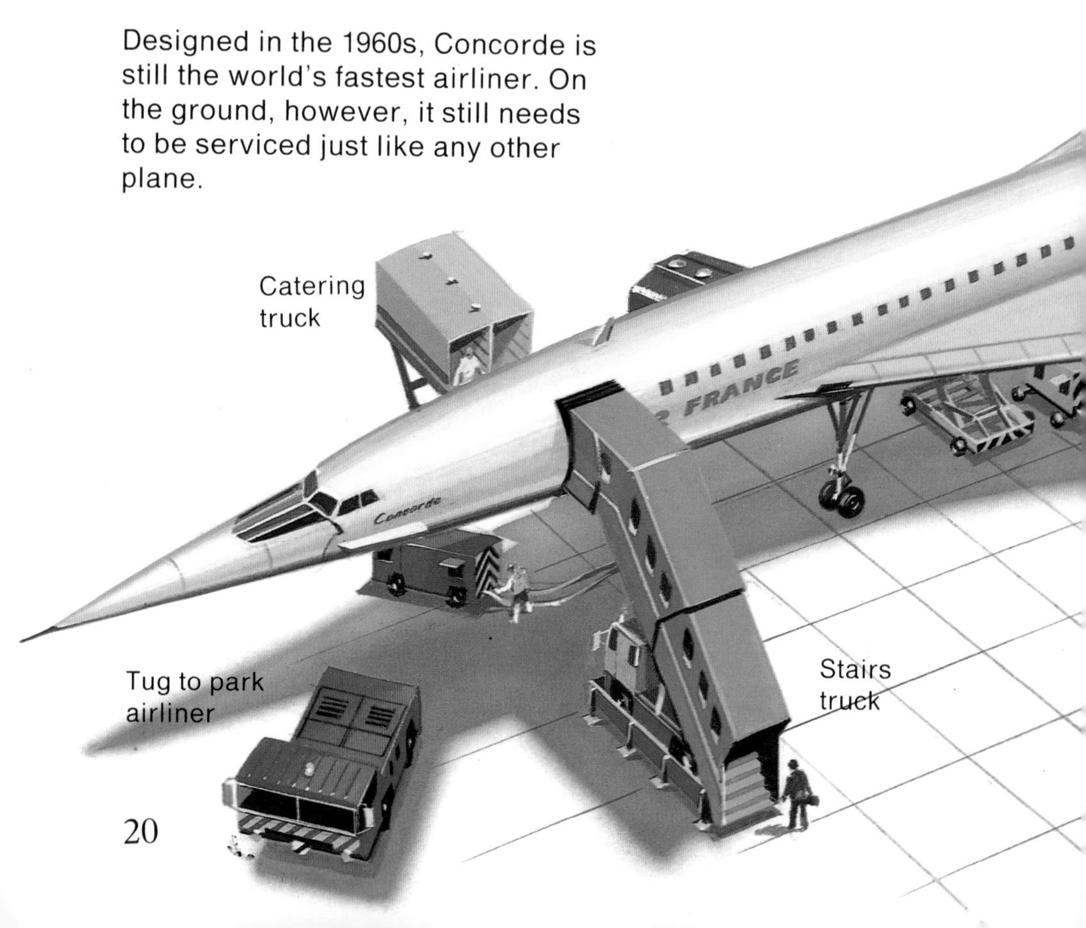

Between flights, the plane's fuel tanks are refilled with kerosene from a tanker truck. Jets burn thousands of litres of fuel each flying hour.

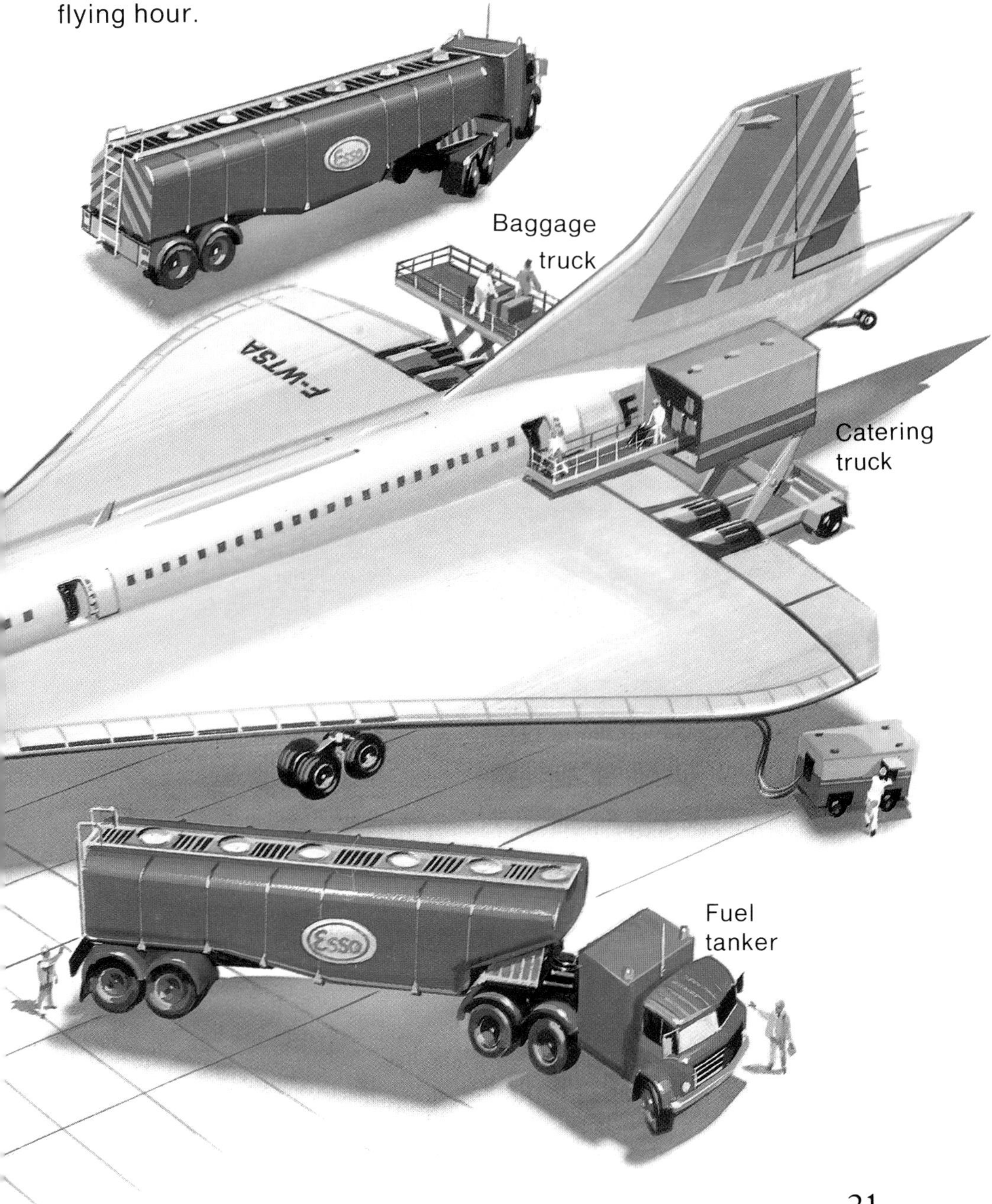

Baggage truck

Catering truck

Fuel tanker

Air-traffic Control

Safety in the air and on the ground is the job of the air-traffic controllers. Through the huge windows of the control tower, they can watch planes on the ground and in the skies near the airport. They also have radar screens, where planes that are too far away to see are tracked as blips of light.

Before leaving the apron (A), the pilot asks permission from the control tower (C). The plane then taxis slowly to near the beginning of the runway (R), where the pilot waits (W) for permission to take off.

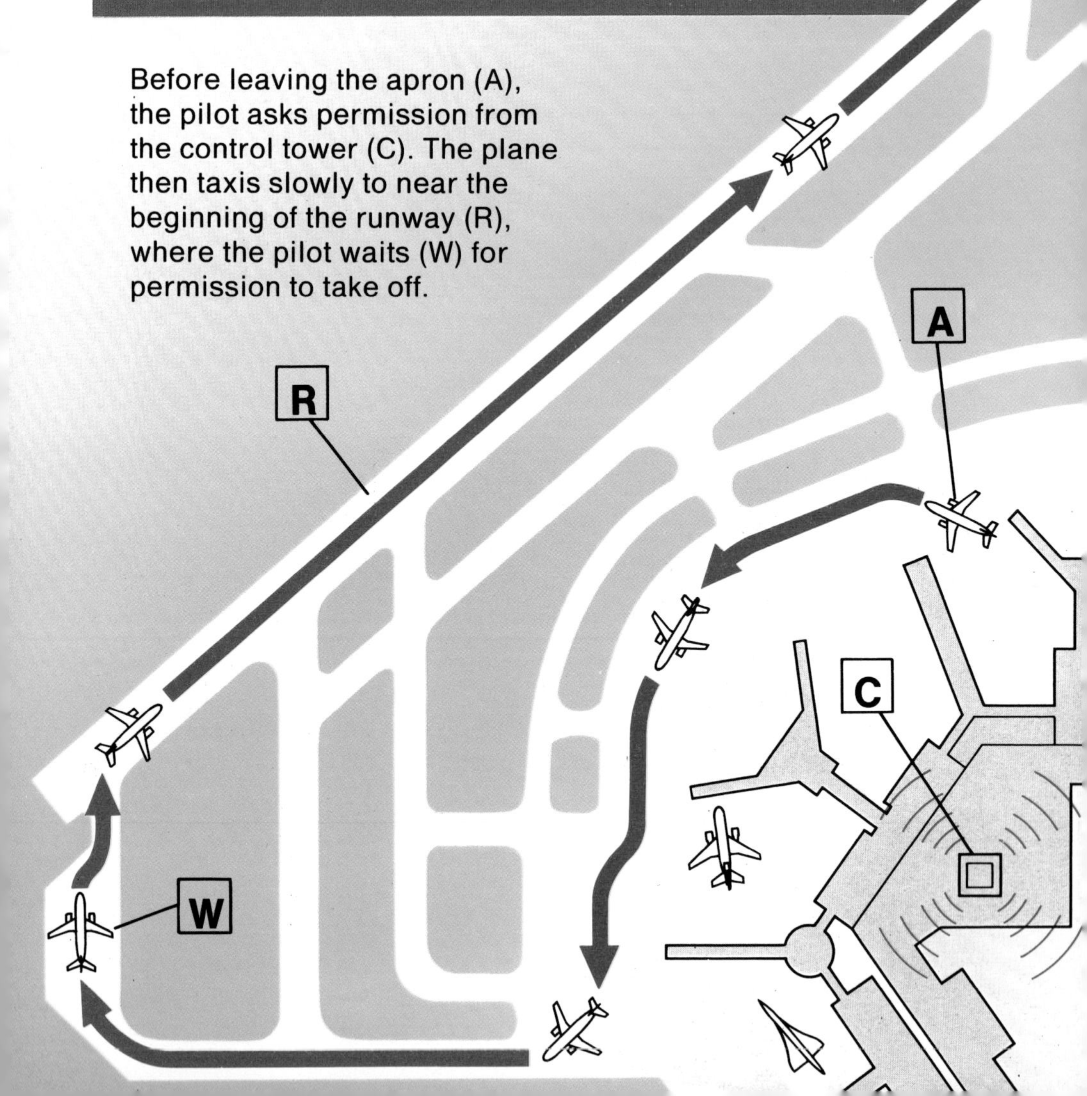

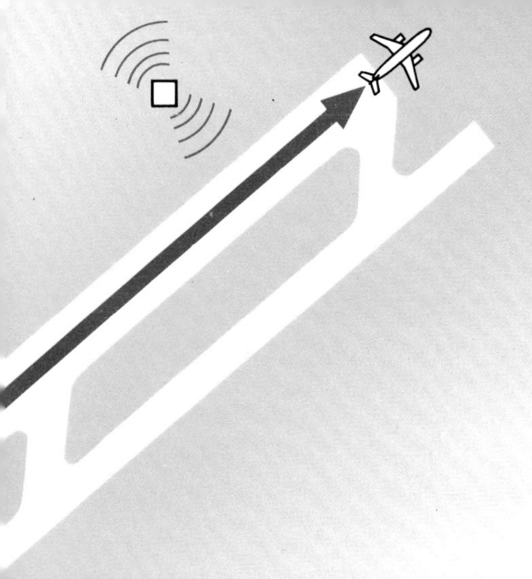

◀ Big jets have to travel a long way to build up enough speed to take off. Runways can be as long as 5 kilometres.

▲ The control tower where the air-traffic controllers work is usually the tallest building in the airport.

TALKING ACROSS THE AIR WAVES

Air-traffic controllers talk to pilots by radio. They give the pilots permission to take off or land, and they tell them which route to fly. In the air, planes travel along special routes called airways.

When a plane's special registration mark is given over the radio, words are used for the letters so that no one mixes up the sounds. Here is the phonetic, or sound, alphabet that is used.

A	ALPHA	**N**	NOVEMBER
B	BRAVO	**O**	OSCAR
C	CHARLIE	**P**	PAPA
D	DELTA	**Q**	QUEBEC
E	ECHO	**R**	ROMEO
F	FOXTROT	**S**	SIERRA
G	GOLF	**T**	TANGO
H	HOTEL	**U**	UNIFORM
I	INDIA	**V**	VICTOR
J	JULIET	**W**	WHISKY
K	KILO	**X**	X-RAY
L	LIMA	**Y**	YANKEE
M	MIKE	**Z**	ZULU

Ground Crew

Many other people work behind the scenes at the airport to keep things running smoothly and safely. The engineers are very important. They have to service the planes and make sure they are safe to fly. The lives of hundreds of passengers depend on this.

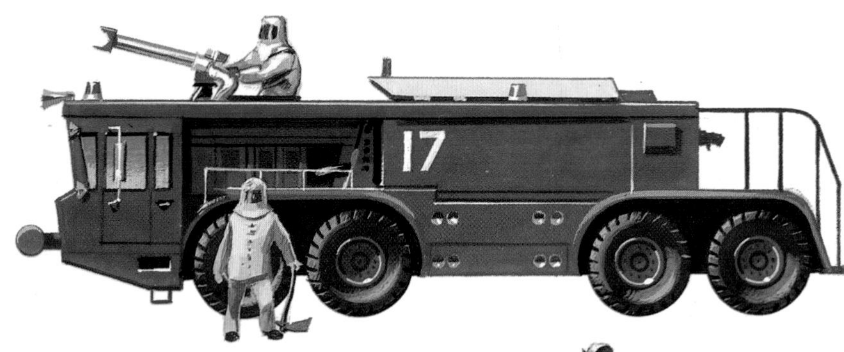

▲ The firefighters' trucks are fitted with powerful guns to smother fires quickly with thick foam.

▼ In winter the runways are kept clear of snow, so that planes can still land safely.

▲ At some airports, fuel is kept in tanks under the apron. Trucks carry hoses to connect the tanks to the aircraft.

GROUND SIGNALS

When an airliner reaches the apron outside the terminal, a marshal is waiting to direct the pilot into the correct parking bay. The plane's engines are very noisy, so marshals wear muffs to protect their ears and use bats to signal to the pilot.

You could use some ping-pong bats, or make some bats from thick cardboard and colour them in to practise these signals for yourself. You could then try guiding a friend on a bicycle into a parking place at home.

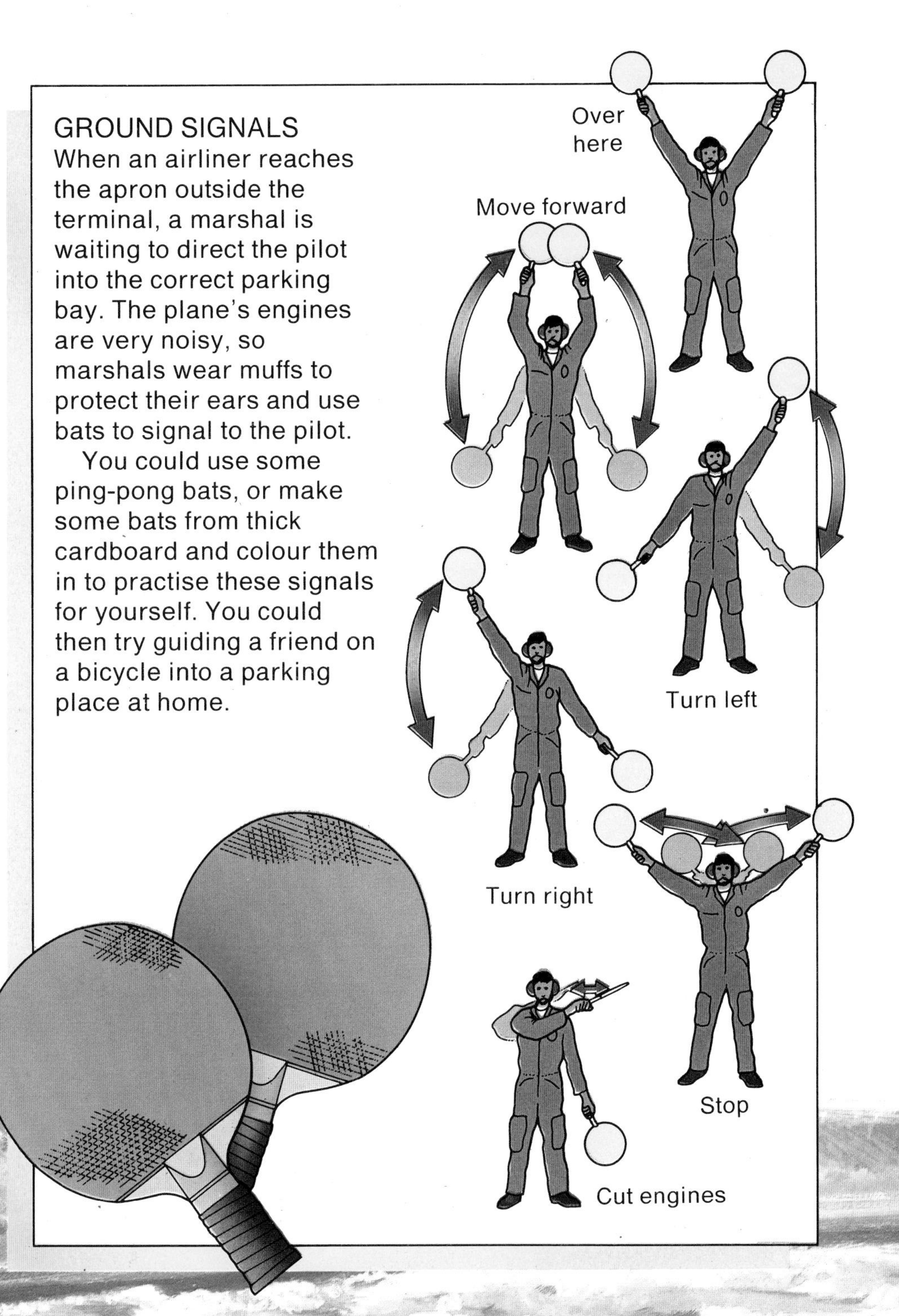

Jet File

Many different planes fly with the world's airlines, but you may need some practice to tell them apart. Look for these airliners when you next visit an airport. There is room here to note where and when you saw them.

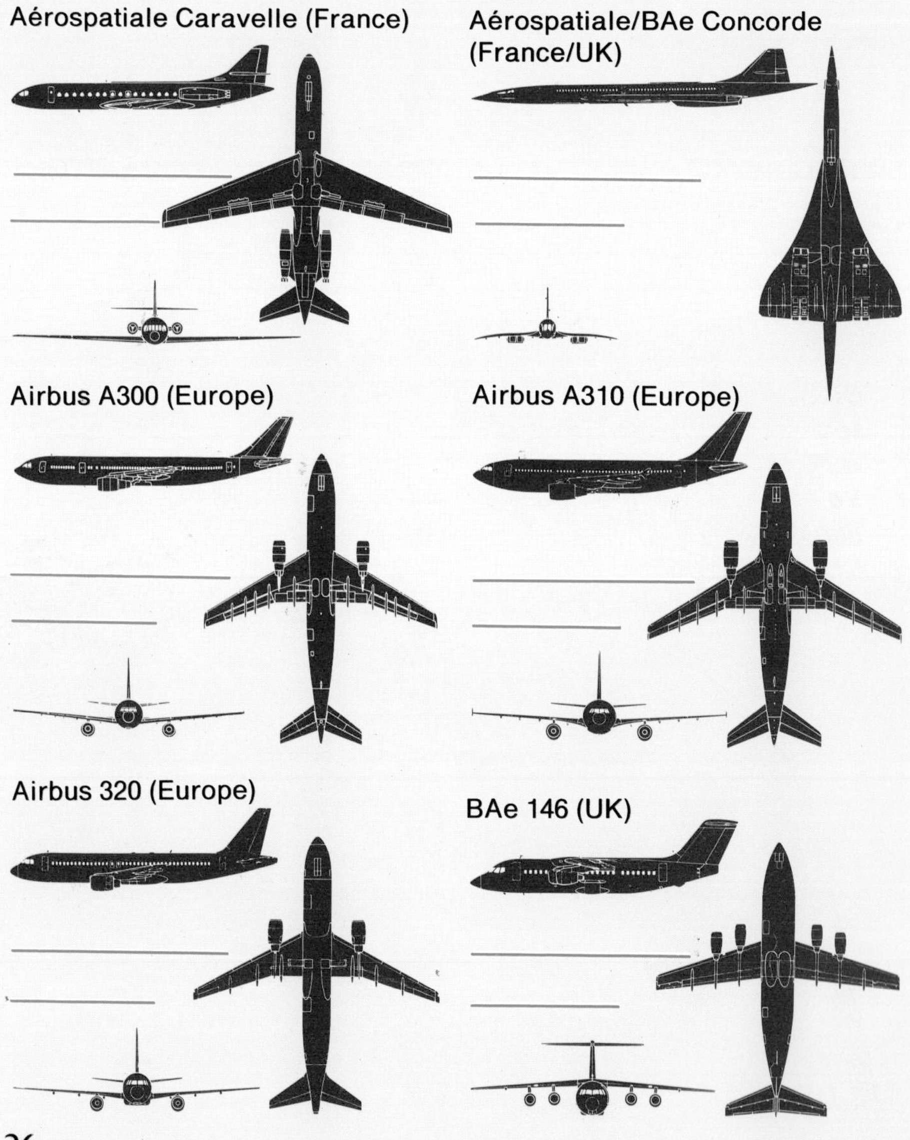

Binoculars will help you spot plane registration marks – look under one wing or on the fuselage near the tail. You could keep a photo and records like these.

Jet File – 2

Boeing 757 (USA)

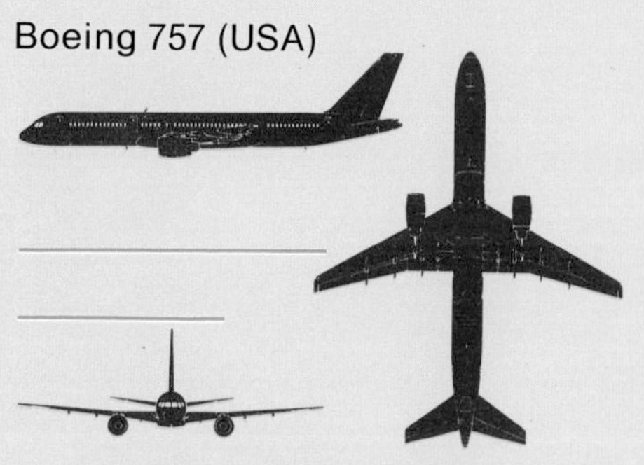

Boeing 767 (USA)

Fokker 100 (Netherlands)

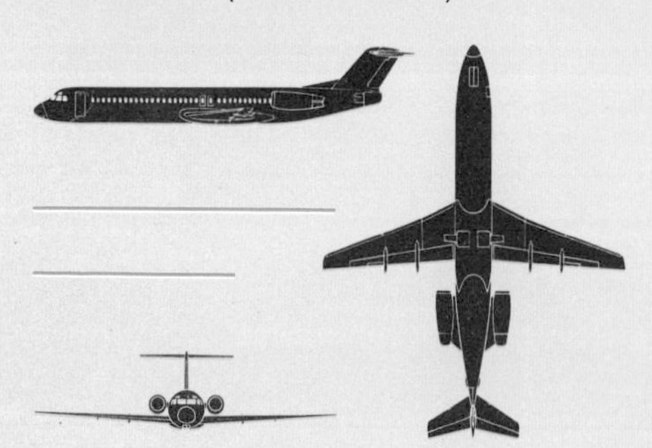

Ilyushin IL-86 (USSR)

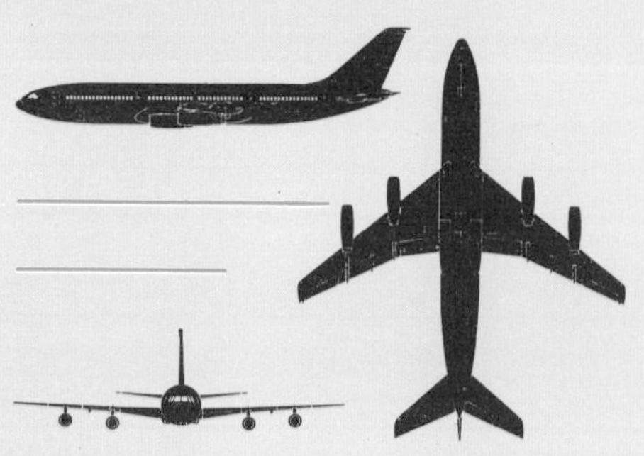

Each airline company has its own special livery, or decoration, for its planes. Coloured stripes are often painted along the fuselage. Usually, there is also a badge on the tail – a flying kangaroo identifies the Australian airline Qantas, for example. Can you identify those shown here?

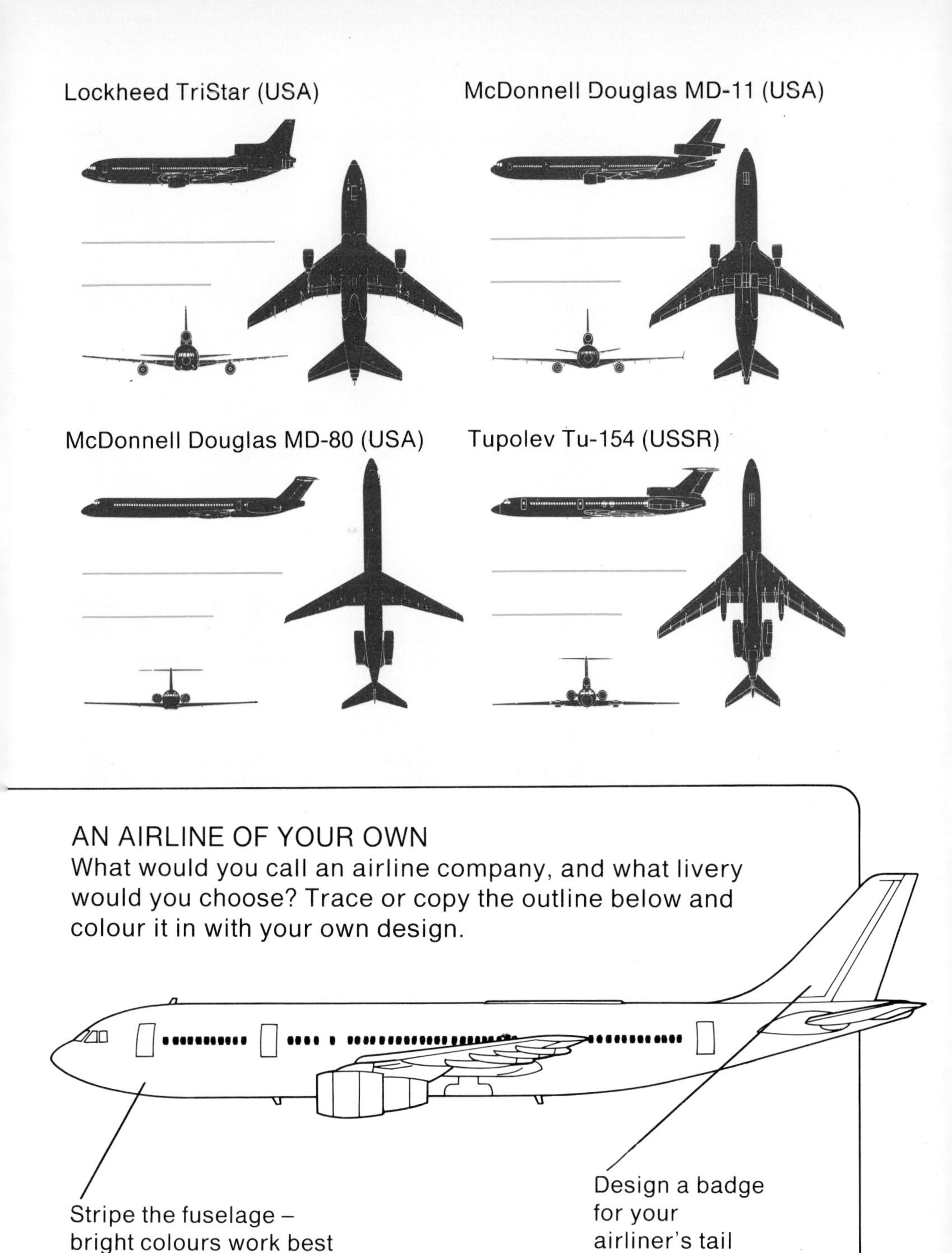

AN AIRLINE OF YOUR OWN

What would you call an airline company, and what livery would you choose? Trace or copy the outline below and colour it in with your own design.

Glossary

Ailerons
Movable parts on the wings which work together to bank an aircraft. When one is up, the other is down.

Airliner
An aircraft that carries passengers.

Airways
The routes that planes fly along in the sky.

Apron
The parking area for aircraft which is outside the airport terminal.

Bank
To roll a plane into a turn.

Boarding
Getting on an aircraft. Passengers are given a pass called a boarding card which they hand in as they board.

Cabin
The area in an airliner where the passengers sit. The people who work here are called cabin crew.

Control column or wheel
Also called a yoke or joystick. The pilot uses it to move the ailerons and elevators to bank or pitch the plane.

Control surfaces
Movable parts on a plane's wings and tail, used for steering. *See* ailerons, elevators and rudder.

Drag
Air resists, or tries to stop, anything moving through it. This resistance is called drag.

Elevators
Movable parts on the tailplane which pitch an aircraft up or down.

Engine
The first aircraft had piston engines to drive propellers. They work rather like car engines and some small planes still use them. Now most big aircraft have jet engines, where thrust comes from a jet of gases.

Flight deck
The area at the front of an airliner where the pilot and other members of the flight crew work.

Fuselage
The main body of an aircraft.

Galley
On airliners and ships, the kitchen is called a galley.

Ground crew
All the people who work on the ground at an airport – engineers, baggage loaders, and so on.

Jet
An aircraft powered by jet engines. *See* engine.

Lift
The upward force that supports the weight of a plane in the air. The wings give lift when they move through the air.

Pitch
To move a plane up or down.

Radar
A way of finding something by bouncing radio waves off it. Radar is used to track planes that are out of eyesight. The Airbus A320 has radar to detect clouds and rain.

Registration mark
Every aircraft has its own registration mark, with a letter code for the country and a number for the plane. The code for British planes is G-A, for example.

Rudder
Movable part on the tail fin which is used to move the plane's nose from side to side, and to steady it against yawing.

Terminal
The main building at an airport, which passengers go through to board planes or after leaving a flight.

Thrust
The force that pushes an aircraft forwards.

Yawing
Yawing is when an aircraft swings from side to side. The pilot uses the rudder to stop this.

Index